FRES SUMMER RECIPES FOR

BREAKFAST

Mirko Lotti

You may have heard the term 'eat seasonally' touted by nutrition experts, foodies, and chefs alike. But what does that mean, and what are the benefits to eating seasonal foods? Also, what are the benefits of consuming foods from this season – summer! We'll discuss in this article.

Eating seasonally basically means including foods in your diet that are grown locally at the same time of year that you buy them. These days, due to importing/exporting practices and refrigerated transportation vehicles, we have an abundance of foods available from all over the world. This of course makes it easier to eat many foods, whether they are in season or not. However, there is more to eating seasonally than just a trendy term; there are many benefits to eating foods that are currently being grown and harvested.

How do you eat healthy?

People often think of healthy eating as dieting. This is not
true. Eating healthy is not just about losing weight, it's
about feeling better both physically and mentally.
Eating healthy is about balance and making sure that your
body is getting the necessary nutrients it needs to function
properly. Healthy eating habits require that people eat
fruits, vegetables, whole grains, fats, proteins, and
starches. Keep in mind that healthy eating requires that
you're mindful of what you eat and drink, but also how
you prepare it. For best results, individuals should avoid
fried or processed foods, as well as foods high in added
sugars and salts.

The fundamentals of healthy eating

While some extreme diets may suggest otherwise, we all
need a balance of protein, fat, carbohydrates, fiber,
vitamins, and minerals in our diets to sustain a healthy
body. You don't need to eliminate certain categories of
food from your diet, but rather select the healthiest
options from each category.

- Weight loss
- Heart Health
- Strong bones and teeth
- Better mood and energy levels
- Improved memory and brain health

Switching to a healthy diet doesn't have to be an all or nothing proposition. You don't have to be perfect, you don't have to completely eliminate foods you enjoy, and you don't have to change everything all at once—that usually only leads to cheating or giving up on your new eating plan.

To set yourself up for success, try to keep things simple. Eating a healthier diet doesn't have to be complicated.Focus on avoiding packaged and processed foods and opting for more fresh ingredients whenever possible.

- Prepare more of your own meals
- Make the right changes
- Read the labels
- Focus on how you feel after eating
- Drink plenty of water

Table of Contents

EAT COLORFUL
EAT HEALTHY

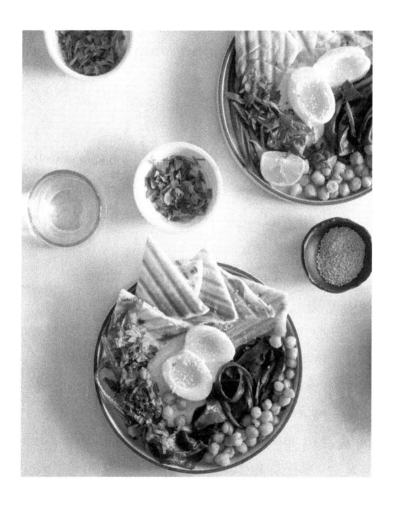

Sweet Potatoes And Apples Mix

Preparation time: 10 minutes

Cooking time: 1 hour and 10 minutes

Servings: 1

Ingredients:

- 2 pounds sweet potatoes
- 2 tablespoons water
- ½ pound apples, cored and chopped
- 1 tablespoon low-fat butter

Directions:

1. Arrange the potatoes on a lined baking sheet, bake in the oven at 400 degrees F for 1 hour, peel them and mash them in your food processor.

2. Put apples in a pot, add the water, bring to a boil over medium heat, reduce temperature, cook for 10 minutes, transfer to a bowl, add

mashed potatoes, stir well and serve for breakfast.

Enjoy!

Nutrition: calories 140, fat 1, fiber 4, carbs 8, protein 6

Pear Breakfast Salad

Preparation time: 10 minutes

Cooking time: 0 minutes

Servings: 4

Ingredients:

- 3 big pears, cored and cut with a spiralizer
- ¾ cup pomegranate seeds
- 5 ounces arugula
- ¾ cup walnuts, roughly chopped

For the vinaigrette:

- 2 tablespoons olive oil
- 1 tablespoon coconut sugar
- 1 teaspoon white sesame seeds
- 2 tablespoons apple cider vinegar
- 1 garlic clove, minced
- Black pepper to the taste

Directions:

1. In a bowl, combine the olive oil with sugar, sesame seeds, vinegar, garlic and pepper and whisk well.
2. In a salad bowl, mix pear with arugula, walnuts and pomegranate seeds, toss, add the vinaigrette, toss and serve for breakfast.

Enjoy!

Nutrition: calories 182, fat 2, fiber 7, carbs 11, protein 7

Breakfast Bulgur Salad

Preparation time: 15 minutes
Cooking time: 0 minutes
Servings: 6

Ingredients:

- 1 and ½ cups hot water
- 1 cup bulgur
- Juice of 1 lime
- 4 tablespoons cilantro, chopped
- ½ cup cranberries, dried
- 1 and ½ teaspoons curry powder
- 1/3 cup almonds, sliced
- ¼ cup green onions, chopped
- ½ cup red bell peppers, chopped
- ½ cup carrots, grated
- 4 tablespoons pepitas
- 1 tablespoon olive oil
- Black pepper to the taste

Directions:

1. Put bulgur into a bowl, add boiling water, cover, leave aside for 15 minutes, fluff bulgur with a fork and transfer to a salad bowl.
2. Add lime juice, cilantro, cranberries, almonds, bell peppers, onions, carrots, curry powder, pepitas, black pepper and the oil, toss and serve for breakfast.

Enjoy!

Nutrition: calories 190, fat 3, fiber 3, carbs 13, protein 10

Black Bean Breakfast Salad

Preparation time: 15 minutes
Cooking time: 0 minutes
Servings: 4

Ingredients:

- 1 and ½ cups canned black beans, no-salt-added, drained and rinsed
- ½ teaspoon garlic powder
- ½ teaspoon smoked paprika
- 2 teaspoons chili powder
- Black pepper to the taste
- 1 teaspoon cumin, ground
- 1 and ½ cups canned chickpeas, no-salt-added, drained and rinsed
- ¼ teaspoon cinnamon powder
- 1 lettuce head, chopped
- 1 red bell pepper, chopped
- 2 tomatoes, chopped

- 1 avocado, pitted, peeled and chopped
- 1 cup corn kernels, chopped

For the salad dressing:

- 2 tablespoons lemon juice
- ¾ cup cashews, soaked and drained
- ½ cup water
- 1 garlic clove, minced
- 1 tablespoon apple cider vinegar
- ½ teaspoon onion powder
- 1 teaspoon chives, chopped
- ½ teaspoon oregano, dried
- 1 teaspoon dill, dried
- 1 teaspoon cumin, ground
- ½ teaspoon smoked paprika

Directions:

1. In your blender, mix cashews with water, 2 tablespoons lemon juice, 1 tablespoon vinegar, 1 garlic clove, ½ teaspoon onion powder, dill, oregano, chives, cumin and ½ teaspoon paprika, blend really well and leave aside for now.

2. In a salad bowl, mix black beans with chili powder, ½ teaspoon garlic powder, ½ teaspoon paprika, chickpeas, cinnamon and black pepper to the taste and stir really well.

3. Add lettuce leaves, tomatoes, corn, avocado and bell peppers, toss everything, drizzle the salad dressing, mix everything again and serve for breakfast.

Nutrition: calories 190, fat 4, fiber 10, carbs 11, protein 11

Chickpeas Breakfast Salad

Preparation time: 10 minutes
Cooking time: 0 minutes
Servings: 2

Ingredients:

- 16 ounces canned chickpeas, no-salt-added, drained and rinsed
- 1 handful baby spinach leaves
- ½ tablespoon lemon juice
- 4 tablespoons olive oil
- 1 teaspoon cumin, ground
- Black pepper to the taste
- ½ teaspoon chili flakes

Directions:

1. In a bowl, mix lemon juice, oil, cumin, black pepper and chili flakes and whisk well.

2. In a salad bowl, mix chickpeas with spinach, add salad dressing, toss to coat and serve for breakfast.

Enjoy!

Nutrition: calories 220, fat 3, fiber 6, carbs 12, protein 8

Mediterranean Breakfast Salad

Preparation time: 10 minutes

Cooking time: 0 minutes

Servings: 4

Ingredients:

- 1 handful kalamata olives, pitted and sliced
- 1-pint cherry tomatoes, halved
- 4 tomatoes, chopped
- 1 and ½ cucumbers, sliced
- 1 red onion, chopped
- 2 tablespoons oregano, chopped
- 1 tablespoon mint, chopped

For the salad dressing:

- 1 teaspoon coconut sugar
- 2 tablespoons balsamic vinegar
- ¼ cup olive oil
- 1 garlic clove, minced

- 2 teaspoons Italian herbs, dried
- Black pepper to the taste

Directions:
1. In a salad bowl, mix cherry tomatoes with tomatoes, olives, cucumbers, onion, mint and oregano and toss
2. In another bowl, mix sugar with vinegar, oil, garlic, dried Italian herbs and black pepper, whisk well, add to your salad, toss to coat and serve for breakfast.

Enjoy!

Nutrition: calories 180, fat 2, fiber 3, carbs 6, protein 9

Easy Veggie Muffins

Preparation time: 10 minutes

Cooking time: 40 minutes

Servings: 4

Ingredients:

- ¾ cup cheddar cheese, shredded
- 1 cup green onion, chopped
- 1 cup tomatoes, chopped
- 1 cup broccoli, chopped
- 2 cups non-fat milk
- 1 cup biscuit ix
- 4 eggs
- Cooking spray
- 1 teaspoon Italian seasoning
- A pinch of black pepper

Directions:

1. Grease a muffin tray with cooking spray and divide broccoli, tomatoes cheese and onions in each muffin cup.
2. In a bowl, combine green onions with milk, biscuit mix, eggs, pepper and Italian seasoning, whisk well and pour into the muffin tray as well.
3. Cook the muffins in the oven at 375 degrees F for 40 minutes, divide them between plates and serve.

Enjoy!

Nutrition: calories 212, fat 2, fiber 3, carbs 12, protein 6

Carrot Muffins

Preparation time: 10 minutes

Cooking time: 30 minutes

Servings: 5

Ingredients:

- 1 and ½ cups whole wheat flour
- ½ cup stevia
- 1 teaspoon baking powder
- ½ teaspoon cinnamon powder
- ½ teaspoon baking soda
- ¼ cup natural apple juice
- ¼ cup olive oil
- 1 egg
- 1 cup fresh cranberries
- 2 carrots, grated
- 2 teaspoons ginger, grated
- ¼ cup pecans, chopped
- Cooking spray

Directions:

1. In a large bowl, combine the flour with the stevia, baking powder, cinnamon and baking soda and stir well.
2. Add apple juice, oil, egg, cranberries, carrots, ginger and pecans and stir really well.
3. Grease a muffin tray with cooking spray, divide the muffin mix, introduce in the oven and cook at 375 degrees F for 30 minutes.
4. Divide the muffins between plates and serve for breakfast.

Enjoy!

Nutrition: calories 212, fat 3, fiber 6, carbs 14, protein 6

Pineapple Oatmeal

Preparation time: 10 minutes

Cooking time: 25 minutes

Servings: 4

Ingredients:

- 2 cups old-fashioned oats
- 1 cup walnuts, chopped
- 2 cups pineapple, cubed
- 1 tablespoon ginger, grated
- 2 cups non-fat milk
- 2 eggs
- 2 tablespoons stevia
- 2 teaspoons vanilla extract

Directions:

1. In a bowl, combine the oats with the pineapple, walnuts and ginger, stir and divide into 4 ramekins.

2. In a bowl, combine the milk with the eggs, stevia and vanilla, whisk well and pour over the oats mix.
3. Introduce in the oven and cook at 400 degrees F for 25 minutes.
4. Serve for breakfast.

Enjoy!

Nutrition: calories 211, fat 2, fiber 4, carbs 14, protein 6

Spinach Muffins

Preparation time: 10 minutes

Cooking time: 30 minutes

Servings: 6

Ingredients:

- 6 eggs
- ½ cup non-fat milk
- 1 cup low-fat cheese, crumbled
- 4 ounces spinach
- ½ cup roasted red pepper, chopped
- 2 ounces prosciutto, chopped
- Cooking spray

Directions:

1. In a bowl, combine the eggs with the milk, cheese, spinach, red pepper and prosciutto and whisk well.

2. Grease a muffin tray with cooking spray, divide the muffin mix, introduce in the oven and bake at 350 degrees F for 30 minutes.
3. Divide between plates and serve for breakfast.

Enjoy!

Nutrition: calories 155, fat 10, fiber 1, carbs 4, protein 10

Chia Seeds Breakfast Mix

Preparation time: 8 hours

Cooking time: 0 minutes

Servings: 4

Ingredients:

- 2 cups old-fashioned oats
- 4 tablespoons chia seeds
- 4 tablespoons coconut sugar
- 3 cups coconut milk
- 1 teaspoon lemon zest, grated
- 1 cup blueberries

Directions:

1. In a bowl, combine the oats with chia seeds, sugar, milk, lemon zest and blueberries, stir, divide into cups and keep in the fridge for 8 hours.
2. Serve for breakfast.

Enjoy!

Nutrition: calories 283, fat 12, fiber 3, carbs 13, protein 8

Breakfast Fruits Bowls

Preparation time: 10 minutes

Cooking time: 0 minutes

Servings: 2

Ingredients:

- 1 cup mango, chopped
- 1 banana, sliced
- 1 cup pineapple, chopped
- 1 cup almond milk

Directions:

1. In a bowl, combine the mango with the banana, pineapple and almond milk, stir, divide into smaller bowls and serve for breakfast.

Enjoy!

Nutrition: calories 182, fat 2, fiber 4, carbs 12, protein 6

Pumpkin Breakfast Cookies

Preparation time: 10 minutes

Cooking time: 25 minutes

Servings: 6

Ingredients:

- 2 cups whole wheat flour
- 1 cup old-fashioned oats
- 1 teaspoon baking soda
- 1 teaspoon pumpkin pie spice
- 15 ounces pumpkin puree
- 1 cup coconut oil, melted
- 1 cup coconut sugar
- 1 egg
- ½ cup pepitas, roasted
- ½ cup cherries, dried

Directions:

1. In a bowl, combine the flour with the oats, baking soda, pumpkin spice, pumpkin puree, oil, sugar, egg, pepitas and cherries, stir well, shape medium cookies out of this mix, arrange them all on a lined baking sheet, introduce in the oven and bake at 350 degrees F for 25 minutes.
2. Serve the cookies for breakfast.

Enjoy!

Nutrition: calories 281, fat 12, fiber 3, carbs 14, protein 6

Veggie Scramble

Preparation time: 10 minutes

Cooking time: 2 minutes

Servings: 1

Ingredients:

- 1 egg
- 1 tablespoon water
- ¼ cup broccoli, chopped
- ¼ cup mushrooms, chopped
- A pinch of black pepper
- 1 tablespoon low-fat mozzarella, shredded
- 1 tablespoon walnuts, chopped
- Cooking spray

Directions:

1. Grease a ramekin with cooking spray, add the egg, water, pepper, mushrooms and broccoli and whisk well.

2. Introduce in the microwave and cook for 2 minutes.

3. Add mozzarella and walnuts on top and serve for breakfast.

Enjoy!

Nutrition: calories 211, fat 2, fiber 4, carbs 12, protein 6

Mushrooms and Turkey Breakfast

Preparation time: 10 minutes

Cooking time: 1 hour and 5 minutes

Servings: 12

Ingredients:

- 8 ounces whole wheat bread, cubed
- 12 ounces turkey sausage, chopped
- 2 cups fat-free milk
- 5 ounces low-fat cheddar, shredded
- 3 eggs
- ½ cup green onions, chopped
- 1 cup mushrooms, chopped
- ½ teaspoon sweet paprika
- A pinch of black pepper
- 2 tablespoons low-fat parmesan, grated

Directions:

1. Spread bread cubes on a lined baking sheet, introduce in the oven and bake at 400 degrees F for 8 minutes.
2. Meanwhile, heat up a pan over medium-high heat, add turkey sausage, stir and brown for 7 minutes.
3. In a bowl, combine the milk with the cheddar, eggs, parmesan, black pepper and paprika and whisk well.
4. Add mushrooms, sausage, bread cubes and green onions, stir, pour into a baking dish, introduce in the oven and bake at 350 degrees F for 50 minutes.
5. Slice, divide between plates and serve for breakfast.

Enjoy!

Nutrition: calories 221, fat 3, fiber 6, carbs 12, protein 6

Delicious Omelet

Preparation time: 10 minutes
Cooking time: 6 minutes
Servings: 2

Ingredients:

- 2 eggs
- 2 tablespoons water
- 1 teaspoon olive oil
- ¼ cup low-fat Mexican cheese, shredded
- ¼ cup chunky salsa
- A pinch of black pepper

Directions:

1. In a bowl, combine the eggs with the water, cheese, salsa and pepper and whisk well.

2. Heat up a pan with the oil over medium-high heat, add the eggs mix, spread into the pan, cook for 3 minutes, flip, cook for 3 more minutes, divide between plates and serve for breakfast.

Enjoy!

Nutrition: calories 221, fat 4, fiber 4, carbs 13, protein 7

Easy Omelet Waffles

Preparation time: 10 minutes

Cooking time: 5 minutes

Servings: 2

Ingredients:

- 4 eggs
- A pinch of black pepper
- 2 tablespoons ham, chopped
- ¼ cup low-fat cheddar, shredded
- 2 tablespoons parsley, chopped
- Cooking spray

Directions:

1. In a bowl, combine the eggs with pepper, ham, cheese and parsley and whisk really well.
2. Grease your waffle iron with cooking spray, add the eggs mix, cook for 4-5 minutes, divide the waffles between plates and serve them for breakfast.

Enjoy!

Nutrition: calories 211, fat 3, fiber 6, carbs 14, protein 8

Jared Omelets

Preparation time: 10 minutes

Cooking time: 6 minutes

Servings: 2

Ingredients:

- Cooking spray
- 2/3 cup low-fat cheddar, shredded
- 4 eggs
- ½ yellow onion, chopped
- ½ cup ham, chopped
- 1 red bell pepper, chopped
- A pinch of black pepper
- 1 tablespoon chives, chopped

Directions:

1. In a bowl, combine the eggs with onion, ham, bell pepper and pepper and whisk well.
2. Grease 2 mason jars with cooking spray, divide the eggs mix, introduce in the oven and bake at 350 degrees F for 6 minutes.
3. Sprinkle the cheese all over and serve for breakfast.

Enjoy!

Nutrition: calories 221, fat 3, fiber 3, carbs 14, protein 7

Mushrooms And Cheese Omelet

Preparation time: 10 minutes

Cooking time: 15 minutes

Servings: 4

Ingredients:

- 2 tablespoons olive oil
- A pinch of black pepper
- 3 ounces mushrooms, sliced
- 1 cup baby spinach, chopped
- 3 eggs, whisked
- 2 tablespoons low-fat cheese, grated
- 1 small avocado, peeled, pitted and cubed
- 1 tablespoons parsley, chopped

Directions:

1. Heat up a pan with the oil over medium-high heat, add mushrooms, stir, cook them for 5 minutes and transfer to a bowl.

2. Heat up the same pan over medium-high heat, add eggs and black pepper, spread into the pan, cook for 7 minutes and transfer to a plate.
3. Spread mushrooms, spinach, avocado and cheese on half of the omelet, fold the other half over this mix, sprinkle parsley on top and serve.

Enjoy!

Nutrition: calories 199, fat 3, fiber 4, carbs 14, protein 6

Egg White Breakfast Mix

Preparation time: 10 minutes

Cooking time: 10 minutes

Servings: 4

Ingredients:

- 1 yellow onion, chopped
- 3 plum tomatoes, chopped
- 10 ounces spinach, chopped
- A pinch of black pepper
- 2 tablespoons water
- 12 egg whites
- Cooking spray

Directions:

1. In a bowl, combine the egg whites with water and pepper and whisk well.
2. Grease a pan with cooking spray, heat up over medium heat, add ¼ of the egg whites, spread into the pan and cook for 2 minutes.
3. Spoon ¼ of the spinach, tomatoes and onion, fold and add to a plate.
4. Repeat with the rest of the egg whites and veggies and serve for breakfast.

Enjoy!

Nutrition: calories 235, fat 4, fiber 7, carbs 14, protein 7

Pesto Omelet

Preparation time: 10 minutes

Cooking time: 6 minutes

Servings: 2

Ingredients:

- 2 teaspoons olive oil
- A handful cherry tomatoes, chopped
- 3 tablespoons pistachio pesto
- A pinch of black pepper
- 4 eggs

Directions:

1. In a bowl, combine the eggs with cherry tomatoes, black pepper and pistachio pesto and whisk well.
2. Heat up a pan with the oil over medium-high heat, add eggs mix, spread into the pan, cook for 3 minutes, flip, cook for 3 minutes more, divide between 2 plates and serve for breakfast.

Enjoy!

Nutrition: calories 199, fat 2, fiber 4, carbs 14, protein 7

Quinoa Bowls

Preparation time: 10 minutes

Cooking time: 20 minutes

Servings: 2

Ingredients:

- 1 peach, sliced
- 1/3 cup quinoa, rinsed
- 2/3 cup low-fat milk
- ½ teaspoon vanilla extract
- 2 teaspoons brown sugar
- 12 raspberries
- 14 blueberries

Directions:

1. In a small pan, combine the quinoa with the milk, sugar and vanilla, stir, bring to a simmer over medium heat, cover the pan, cook for 20 minutes and flip with a fork.
2. Divide this mix into 2 bowls, top each with raspberries and blueberries and serve for breakfast.

Enjoy!

Nutrition: calories 177, fat 2, fiber 4, carbs 9, protein 8

Strawberry Sandwich

Preparation time: 10 minutes

Cooking time: 0 minutes

Servings: 4

Ingredients:

- 8 ounces low-fat cream cheese, soft
- 1 tablespoon stevia
- 1 teaspoon lemon zest, grated
- 4 whole wheat English muffins, halved and toasted
- 2 cups strawberries, sliced

Directions:

1. In your food processor, combine the cream cheese with the stevia and lemon zest and pulse well.
2. Spread 1 tablespoon of this mix on 1 muffin half and top with some of the sliced strawberries.

3. Repeat with the rest of the muffin halves and serve for breakfast.

Enjoy!

Nutrition: calories 211, fat 3, fiber 4, carbs 8, protein 4

Apple Quinoa Muffins

Preparation time: 10 minutes

Cooking time: 35 minutes

Servings: 4

Ingredients:

- ½ cup natural, unsweetened applesauce
- 1 cup banana, peeled and mashed
- 1 cup quinoa
- 2 and ½ cups old-fashioned oats
- ½ cup almond milk
- 2 tablespoons stevia
- 1 teaspoon vanilla extract
- 1 cup water
- Cooking spray
- 1 teaspoon cinnamon powder
- 1 apple, cored, peeled and chopped

Directions:

1. Put the water in a small pan, bring to a simmer over medium heat, add quinoa, cook for 15 minutes, fluff with a fork and transfer to a bowl.
2. Add banana, applesauce, oats, almond milk, stevia, vanilla, cinnamon and apple, stir, divide into a muffin pan greases with cooking spray, introduce in the oven and bake at 375 degrees F for 20 minutes.
3. Serve for breakfast.

Enjoy!

Nutrition: calories 200, fat 3, fiber 4, carbs 14, protein 7

Amazing Quinoa Hash Browns

Preparation time: 10 minutes

Cooking time: 25 minutes

Servings: 2

Ingredients:

- 1/3 cup quinoa
- 2/3 cup water
- 1 and ½ cups potato, peeled and grated
- 1 eggs
- A pinch of black pepper
- 1 tablespoon olive oil
- 2 green onions, chopped

Directions:

1. Put the water in a small pan, bring to a simmer over medium heat, add quinoa, stir, cover, cook for 15 minutes and fluff with a fork.
2. IN a bowl, combine the quinoa with potato, egg, green onions and pepper and stir well.
3. Heat up a pan with the oil over medium-high heat, add quinoa hash browns, cook for 5 minutes on each side, divide between 2 plates and serve for breakfast.

Enjoy!

Nutrition: calories 191, fat 3, fiber 8, carbs 14, protein 7

Quinoa Breakfast Bars

Preparation time: 2 hours
Cooking time: 0 minutes
Servings: 6

Ingredients:

- ½ cup fat-free peanut butter
- 2 tablespoons coconut sugar
- 1 teaspoon vanilla extract
- ½ teaspoon cinnamon powder
- 1 cup quinoa flakes
- 1/3 cup coconut, flaked
- 2 tablespoons unsweetened chocolate chips

Directions:

1. In a large bowl, combine the peanut butter with sugar, vanilla, cinnamon, quinoa, coconut and chocolate chips, stir well, spread on the bottom of a lined baking sheet, press well, cut

in 6 bars, keep in the fridge for 2 hours, divide between plates and serve.

Enjoy!

Nutrition: calories 182, fat 4, fiber 4, carbs 13, protein 11

Quinoa Quiche

Preparation time: 10 minutes

Cooking time: 45 minutes

Servings: 4

Ingredients:

- 1` cup quinoa, cooked
- 3 ounces spinach, chopped
- 1 cup fat-free ricotta cheese
- 3 eggs
- 1 and ½ teaspoons garlic powder
- 2/3 cup low-fat parmesan, grated

Directions:

1. In a bowl, combine the quinoa with the spinach, ricotta, eggs, garlic powder and parmesan, whisk well, pour into a lined pie pan, introduce in the oven and bake at 355 degrees F for 45 minutes.

2. Cool the quiche down, slice and serve for breakfast.

Enjoy!

Nutrition: calories 201, fat 2, fiber 4, carbs 12, protein 7

Quinoa Breakfast Parfaits

Preparation time: 10 minutes

Cooking time: 20 minutes

Servings: 4

Ingredients:

For the crumble:

- 1 tablespoon coconut oil, melted
- ½ cup rolled oats
- 2 teaspoons coconut sugar
- 1 tablespoon walnuts, chopped
- 1 teaspoon cinnamon powder

For the apple mix:

- 4 apples, cored, peeled and chopped
- 1 teaspoon vanilla extract
- 1 teaspoon cinnamon powder
- 1 tablespoon coconut sugar
- 2 tablespoons water

For the quinoa mix:

- 1 cup quinoa, cooked

- 1 teaspoon cinnamon powder
- 2 cups nonfat yogurt

Directions:

1. In a bowl, combine the coconut oil with the rolled water, 2 teaspoons coconut sugar, walnuts and 1 teaspoon cinnamon, stir, spread on a lined baking sheet, cook at 350 degrees F , bake for 10 minutes and leave aside to cool down.
2. In a small pan, combine the apples with the vanilla, 1 teaspoon cinnamon, 1 tablespoon coconut sugar and the water, stir, cook over medium heat for 10 minutes and take off heat.
3. In a bowl, combine the quinoa with 1 teaspoon cinnamon and 2 cups yogurt and stir.
4. Divide the quinoa mix into bowls, then divide the apple compote and top with the crumble mix.
5. Serve for breakfast.

Enjoy!

Nutrition: calories 188, fat 3, fiber 6, carbs 12, protein 7

Breakfast Quinoa Cakes

Preparation time: 10 minutes

Cooking time: 30 minutes

Servings: 4

Ingredients:

- 1 cup quinoa
- 2 cups cauliflower, chopped
- 1 and ½ cups chicken stock
- ½ cup low-fat cheddar, shredded
- ½ cup low-fat parmesan, grated
- 1 egg
- A pinch of black pepper
- 2 tablespoons canola oil

Directions:

1. In a pot, combine the quinoa with the cauliflower, stock and pepper, stir, bring to a simmer over medium heat and cook for 20 minutes/

2. Add cheddar and the eggs, stir well, shape medium cakes out of this mix and dredge them in the parmesan.

3. Heat up a pan with the oil over medium-high heat, add the quinoa cakes. cook for 4-5 minutes on each side, divide between plates and serve for breakfast.

Enjoy!

Nutrition: calories 199, fat 3, fiber 4, carbs 8, carbs 14, protein 6

Easy Quinoa Pancakes

Preparation time: 10 minutes
Cooking time: 6 minutes
Servings: 8

Ingredients:

- ½ cup unsweetened applesauce
- 2 tablespoons coconut sugar
- ½ cup nonfat milk
- 1 tablespoon lemon juice
- 1 teaspoon baking soda
- 1 and ½ cups quinoa flour

Directions:

1. In your food processor, combine the applesauce with the sugar, milk, lemon juice, baking soda and quinoa and pulse well.
2. Heat up a pan over medium heat, spoon some of the pancake batter, spread into the pan, cook

for 3 minutes on each side and transfer to a plate.

3. Repeat with the rest of the pancake batter, divide the pancakes between plates and serve for breakfast.

Enjoy!

Nutrition: calories 188, fat 3, fiber 6, carbs 13, protein 6

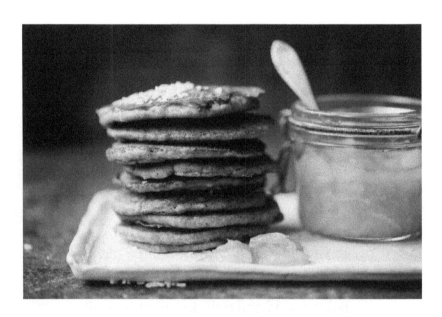

Quinoa And Egg Muffins

Preparation time: 10 minutes

Cooking time: 30 minutes

Servings: 3

Ingredients:

- 1/3 cup quinoa, cooked
- 1 zucchini, chopped
- 2 eggs
- 4 egg whites
- ½ cup low-fat feta cheese, shredded
- A pinch of black pepper
- A splash of hot sauce
- Cooking spray

Directions:

1. In a bowl, combine the quinoa with the zucchini, eggs, egg whites, cheese, black pepper and hot sauce, whisk well and divide into 6 muffin cups greased with the cooking spray.
2. Bake the muffins in the oven at 350 degrees F for 30 minutes.
3. Divide the muffins between plates and serve for breakfast.

Enjoy!

Nutrition: calories 221, fat 7, fiber 2, carbs 13, protein 14

Apple And Quinoa Breakfast Bake

Preparation time: 10 minutes

Cooking time: 10 minutes

Servings: 6

Ingredients:

- 1 cup quinoa, cooked
- ¼ teaspoon olive oil
- 2 teaspoons coconut sugar
- 2 apples, cored, peeled and chopped
- 1 teaspoon cinnamon powder
- ½ cup almond milk

Directions:

1. Grease a ramekin with the oil, add quinoa, apples, sugar, cinnamon and almond milk, stir, introduce in the oven, bake at 350 degrees F for 10 minutes, divide into bowls and serve.

Enjoy!

Nutrition: calories 199, fat 2, fiber 7, carbs 14, protein 8

Quinoa Patties

Preparation time: 10 minutes

Cooking time: 20 minutes

Servings: 6

Ingredients:

- 2 and ½ cups quinoa, cooked
- A pinch of black pepper
- 4 eggs, whisked
- 1 yellow onion, chopped
- ¼ cup chives, chopped
- 1/3 cup low-fat parmesan, grated
- 3 garlic cloves, minced
- 1 cup whole wheat bread crumbs
- 1 tablespoon olive oil

Directions:

1. In a large bowl, combine the quinoa with black pepper, eggs, onion, chives, parmesan, garlic and bread crumbs, stir well and shape medium patties out of this mix.
2. Heat up a pan with the oil over medium-high heat, add quinoa patties, cook them for 10 minutes on each side, divide them between plates and serve for breakfast.

Enjoy!

Nutrition: calories 201, fat 3, fiber 4, carbs 14, protein 8

Peanut Butter Smoothie

Preparation time: 10 minutes

Cooking time: 0 minutes

Servings: 2

Ingredients:

- 2 tablespoons peanut butter
- 2 cups non-fat milk
- 2 bananas, peeled and chopped

Directions:

1. In your blender, combine the peanut butter with the milk and bananas, pulse well, divide into 2 glasses and serve.

Enjoy!

Nutrition: calories176, fat 4, fiber 6, carbs 14, protein 7

Yogurt Peanut Butter Mix

Preparation time: 10 minutes
Cooking time: 0 minutes
Servings: 3

Ingredients:

- 6 ounces nonfat yogurt
- 2 tablespoons red grapes, halved
- 4 teaspoons grape jelly
- 1 tablespoon fat-free peanut butter
- 1 teaspoons peanuts, chopped

Directions:

1. In a bowl, combine the yogurt with the grapes, grape jelly, peanut butter and peanuts, toss well, divide into small cups and serve for breakfast.

Enjoy!

Nutrition: calories 187, fat 2, fiber 3, carbs 6, protein 8

Slow Cooked Oatmeal

Preparation time: 10 minutes

Cooking time: 8 hours

Servings: 3

Ingredients:

- 4 cups nonfat milk
- 2 cups steel cut pats
- 4 cups water
- 1/3 cup raisins
- 1/3 cup cherries, dried
- 1/3 cup apricots, dried and chopped
- 1 teaspoon cinnamon powder

Directions:

1. In your slow cooker, combine the milk with the oats, water, raisins, cherries, apricots and cinnamon, stir, cover, cook on Low for 8 hours, divide into bowls and serve for breakfast.

Enjoy!

Nutrition: calories 171, fat 3, fiber 6, carbs 15, protein 7

Salmon Breakfast Salad

Preparation time: 10 minutes
Cooking time: 0 minutes
Servings: 2

Ingredients:

- 3 tablespoons nonfat yogurt
- 1 teaspoon horseradish sauce
- 1 tablespoon dill, chopped
- 1 teaspoon lemon juice
- 4 ounces smoked salmon, boneless, skinless and torn
- 3 ounces salad greens
- 2 ounces cherry tomatoes, halved
- 2 ounces black olives, pitted and sliced

Directions:

1. In a salad bowl, combine the salmon with salad greens, tomatoes and black olives.

2. In another bowl, combine the yogurt with horseradish, dill and lemon juice, whisk well, pour over the salad, toss well and serve for breakfast.

Enjoy!

Nutrition: calories 177, fat 4, fiber 7, carbs 14, protein 8

Banana And Pear Breakfast Salad

Preparation time: 10 minutes

Cooking time: 0 minutes

Servings: 2

Ingredients:

- 1 banana, peeled and sliced
- 1 Asian pear, cored and cubed
- Juice of ½ lime
- ½ teaspoon cinnamon powder
- 2 ounces pepitas, toasted

Directions:

1. In a bowl, combine the banana with the pear, lime juice, cinnamon and pepitas, toss, divide between small plates and serve for breakfast.

Enjoy!

Nutrition: calories 188, fat 2, fiber 3, carbs 5, protein 7

Simple Plum And Avocado Salad

Preparation time: 10 minutes
Cooking time: 0 minutes
Servings: 3

Ingredients:

- 2 avocados, peeled, pitted and cubed
- 4 plums, stones removed and cubed
- 1 cup cilantro, chopped
- 1 garlic clove, minced
- Juice of 1 lemon
- A drizzle of olive oil
- 1 red chili pepper, minced

Directions:

1. In a salad bowl, combine the avocados with plums, cilantro, garlic, lemon juice, oil and chili pepper, toss well, divide between plates and serve for breakfast.

Enjoy!

Nutrition: calories 212, fat 2, fiber 4, carbs 14, protein 11

Cherries Oatmeal

Preparation time: 10 minutes

Cooking time: 15 minutes

Servings: 6

Ingredients:

- 2 cups old-fashioned oats
- 6 cups water
- 1 cup almond milk
- 1 teaspoon cinnamon powder
- 1 teaspoon vanilla extract
- 2 cups cherries, pitted and sliced

Directions:

1. In a small pot, combine the oats with the water, milk, cinnamon, vanilla and cherries, toss, bring to a simmer over medium-high heat, cook for 15 minutes, divide into bowls and serve for breakfast.

Enjoy!

Nutrition: calories 180, fat 4, fiber 4, carbs 9, protein 7

Orange And Apricots Oatmeal

Preparation time: 10 minutes

Cooking time: 15 minutes

Servings: 4

Ingredients:

- 1 and ½ cups water
- 1 cup steel cut oats
- 1 cup orange juice
- 2 tablespoons apricots, dried and chopped
- 2 tablespoons coconut sugar
- 2 tablespoons pecans, chopped
- ¼ teaspoon cinnamon powder

Directions:

1. In a small pot, combine the oats with the water, orange juice, apricots, sugar, cinnamon and pecans, stir, bring to a simmer over medium heat, cook for 15 minutes, divide into bowls and serve for breakfast.

Enjoy!

Nutrition: calories 190, fat 3, fiber 6, carbs 8, protein 5

Cinnamon Pear Oatmeal

Preparation time: 10 minutes
Cooking time: 15 minutes
Servings: 3

Ingredients:

- 3 cups water
- 1 cup steel cut oats
- 1 tablespoon cinnamon powder
- 1 cup pear, cored, peeled and cubed

Directions:

1. In a small pot, combine the water with the oats, cinnamon and pear, toss, bring to a simmer over medium heat, cook for 15 minutes, divide into bowls and serve for breakfast.

Enjoy!

Nutrition: calories 171, fat 2, fiber 5, carbs 11, protein 6

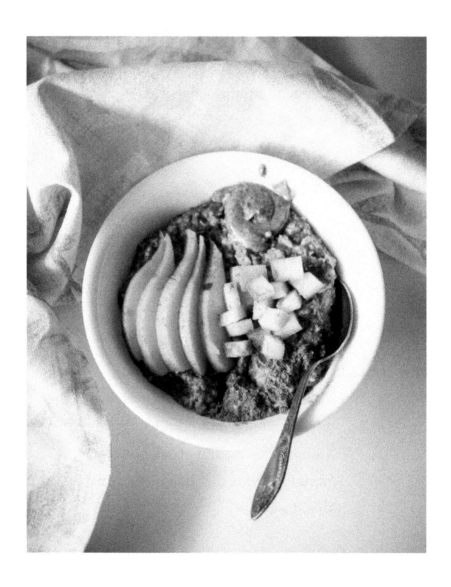

Banana And Walnuts Bowls

Preparation time: 10 minutes

Cooking time: 15 minutes

Servings: 4

Ingredients:

- 2 cups water
- 1 cup steel cut oats
- 1 cup almond milk
- ¼ cup walnuts, chopped
- 2 tablespoons chia seeds
- 2 bananas, peeled and mashed
- 1 teaspoon vanilla extract

Directions:

1. In a small pot, combine the water with the oats, milk, walnuts, chia seeds, bananas and vanilla, toss, bring to a simmer over medium

heat, cook for 15 minutes, divide into bowls and serve for breakfast.

Enjoy!

Nutrition: calories 162, fat 4, fiber 6, carbs 11, protein 4

Parsley Omelet

Preparation time: 10 minutes

Cooking time: 6 minutes

Servings: 6

Ingredients:

- 2 tablespoons almond milk
- A pinch of black pepper
- 6 eggs, whisked
- 2 tablespoons parsley, chopped
- 1 tablespoon low-fat cheddar cheese, shredded
- 2 teaspoons olive oil

Directions:

1. In a bowl, mix the eggs with the milk, black pepper, parsley and cheese and whisk well.
2. Heat up a pan with the oil over medium-high heat, add the eggs mix, spread into the pan, cook for 3 minutes, flip, cook for 3 minutes more, divide between plates and serve for breakfast.

Enjoy!

Nutrition: calories 200, fat 4, fiber 6, carb 13, protein 9

Cheddar Baked Eggs

Preparation time: 10 minutes

Cooking time: 15 minutes

Servings: 4

Ingredients:

- 4 eggs
- 4 slices low-fat cheddar
- 2 spring onions, chopped
- 1 tablespoon olive oil
- A pinch of black pepper
- 1 tablespoon cilantro, chopped

Directions:

1. Grease 4 ramekins with the oil, sprinkle green onions in each, crack an egg in each ramekins and top with cilantro and cheddar cheese.
2. Introduce in the oven and bake at 375 degrees F for 15 minutes.

3. Serve for breakfast.

Enjoy!

Nutrition: calories 199, fat 3, fiber 7, carbs 11, protein 5

Hash Brown Mix

Preparation time: 10 minutes

Cooking time: 30 minutes

Servings: 6

Ingredients:

- Cooking spray
- 6 eggs
- 2 cups hash browns
- ¼ cup non-fat milk
- ½ cup fat-free cheddar cheese, shredded
- 1 small yellow onion, chopped
- A pinch of black pepper
- ½ green bell pepper, chopped
- ½ red bell pepper, chopped

Directions:

1. Heat up a pan greased with cooking spray over medium-high heat, add onions, green

and red bell pepper, stir and cook for 4-5 minutes.

2. Add hash browns and black pepper, stir and cook for 5 minutes more.

3. In a bowl, combine the eggs with milk and cheese, whisk well, pour over the mix from the pan, introduce in the oven and bake at 380 degrees F for 20 minutes.

4. Slice, divide between plates and serve.

Enjoy!

Nutrition: calories 221, fat 4, fiber 5, carbs 14, protein 6

Peaches Mix

Preparation time: 10 minutes
Cooking time: 5 minutes
Servings: 4

Ingredients:
- 6 small peaches, cored and cut into wedges
- ¼ cup coconut sugar
- 2 tablespoons non-fat butter
- ¼ teaspoon almond extract

Directions:
1. In a small pan, combine the peaches with sugar, butter and almond extract, toss, cook over medium-high heat for 5 minutes, divide into bowls and serve for breakfast.

Enjoy!

Nutrition: calories 198, fat 2, fiber 6, carbs 11, protein 8

Cinnamon Brown Rice Pudding

Preparation time: 10 minutes

Cooking time: 25 minutes

Servings: 4

Ingredients:

- 1 cup brown rice
- 1 and ½ cups water
- 1 tablespoon vanilla extract
- 1 tablespoon cinnamon powder
- 1 tablespoon non-fat butter
- ½ cup coconut cream, unsweetened

Directions:

1. In a pot, combine the rice with the water, vanilla, cinnamon, butter and cream, stir, bring to a simmer over medium heat, cook for 25 minutes, divide into bowls and serve for breakfast.

Enjoy!

Nutrition: calories 182, fat 4, fiber 7, carbs 11, protein 6

THANK YOU

Thank you for choosing *Fresh Summer Recipes for Breakfast* for improving your cooking skills! I hope you enjoyed making the recipes as much as tasting them! If you're interested in learning new recipes and new meals to cook, go and check out the other books of the series.

Lightning Source UK Ltd.
Milton Keynes UK
UKHW020654040621
384928UK00011B/869